I Am With You
In All You Feel and Need

by Brooke Summers-Perry

For Chase, Link, and Scout.
For *all* the kids who are waking up their parents, teachers, and clergy.
To the nonviolent revolutionaries that dare to understand, know,
and love themselves enough to dare to understand, know
and love everyone else for who they are.
For the kids that keep asking the why questions.
For all those who accept that we are doing the best we can.
For all those daring enough to be who they are and love who they love.
For the everyday moments that make memories.
For all of us that want to find our way with integrity, respect, love,
equality, competence, community, connection, and contribution.

For each of us........equally.

In memory of my co-workers who passed into full unity years ago.
To Amy: the illustrations that were found in your desk have never left my heart.
To Diana: you lived your short life in such a way that your memory continues
to be a spiritual guide. Because of the two of you, my mind and heart were open
to the possibility of writing and illustrating a children's book.
Even if this book isn't seen outside our house, it has worked its magic here in
my heart and in the heart connection with our kids.

Copyright 2014 Brooke Summers-Perry
www.key2peace.com
All rights reserved. No part of this publication may be reproduced.

This book refers to parenting with Compassionate Communication, also known as *Nonviolent Communication (NVC)*, based on the work of Marshall Rosenberg, PhD..

Some basic principles of *NVC*:
We all have the same set of needs (values).
Every person's needs matter equally.
Our perception alone determines our sense of fulfillment of each need.
We use different strategies to get our needs met.
Conflict is a result of strategies clashing with other strategies.
Our feelings signal whether or not our needs are met.
We have a better chance of connecting with our own needs
and others' needs, when we differentiate our judging thoughts
from what we can objectively observe.

Resources:

cnvc.org - Books, CDs, webinars, and other *Nonviolent Communication (NVC)* resources based on the work of Marshall Rosenberg, PhD and others all over the world who are spreading the gift in this work.

Other *NVC* websites with great resources:
houstonnvc.org
baynvc.org
radicalcompassion.com

The author's website
key2peace.com, includes tools, practices, and reflections on the author's experience with compassionate communication (*NVC*) in parenting, partnering, and spirituality.

When we go to the doctor you tug, pull, and scream.

Are you saying you're scared?
Is that what you mean?

I hold you and tell it's ok to cry.

We're here for your safety.

Does it help to know why?

How about some **adventure** and rescuing duties?

Will you bring me three green bean beauties?

You can carry them **proudly**, do your part,

and bring them to safety in our royal cart.

When it's time to put on your shirt, pants, and shoes,

are you running away **mad** because you want to **choose**?

If I put your clothes where you can pick

can you get yourself dressed really quick?

When you keep on

hey mama,
hey mama,
hey mama
heying,

Are you **frustrated** because I don't hear what you're saying?

What if I bend down and enter your space? Will you be more **heard** if I look at your face?

When your friends played without you and you stopped with a stare,

were you feeling really sad because it seemed so unfair?

Did you want to be part of their group when they played?

Were you wanting some **fairness** at the park that day?

"Mama, Mama! Give me something to do.

I know I can do it! I want **to help** you!"

It seems you're **excited** and wanting a chore.

How would you like to sweep up the floor?

When we get to the park you take off in a race.

Are you **happy** to be in a wide open **space**?

Your safety matters.
It is important to wait.

Let's hold hands until we get through the gate.

I see that you're drawing on your new floor.

I'll get you the paper I bought at the store.

Does it make you feel **glad** to explore **creativity**?

Maybe someday you'll make a book with me.

When it's time for bed and you yell NO, NO, NO!

Do you want to be **close**?
Is it **lonely** to go?

Would you rather cuddle and read for a bit?

Get us some books.
Come closer and sit.

feelings:	values:
scared	safety
proudly	adventure
mad	to choose
frustrated	to be heard
sad	fairness
excited	to help
happy	space
glad	creativity
lonely	to be close

The author is a student of Compassionate Communication (nvc). Her three children, Chase, Link, and Scout are her best teachers.

Her reflections and insights are available at spiritualspark-asif.blogspot.com

I'm With You In All That You Feel and Need.
copyright Brooke Summers-Perry 2014

I Am With You
In All You Feel and Need
copyright 2014
Brooke Summers-Perry

www.ingramcontent.com/pod-product-compliance
Lightning Source LLC
Chambersburg PA
CBHW042129040426
42450CB00002B/125